Notebook

Jillian P. Hersey

Made in the USA
Las Vegas, NV
28 April 2022

48132275R00057